AN INTRODUCTION TO
Auckland Museum

Photographs by Brian Brake and Lau Wai Man
Text by Stuart Park

Published by
Auckland Institute and Museum 1986

CONTENTS

Auckland Museum is one of New Zealand's leading museums, with a proud history and magnificent collections. This book introduces the visitor to those collections, through Brian Brake's wonderful photographs and an informative text by Museum Director Stuart Park. We hope the book will bring pleasure to our many visitors and act as a reminder of the treasures of the Museum.

Russell Thomas

Russell Thomas
President, Auckland Institute and Museum

This superb carving was the waharoa or gateway to Pukeroa, the pa of Ngati Whakaue that stood until the 1840s on the hill where Rotorua Hospital now stands. The carving shows an important ancestor and his descendants. The remarkable polychrome paint has recently been revealed and restored by Auckland Museum conservators. 160 Mitchelson

INTRODUCTION

Auckland Museum was established and opened to the public in 1852, in a small cottage in what are now the grounds of the University of Auckland. The Museum was under the control of the Auckland Provincial Government. The aim of the new Museum was to illustrate the natural history and the raw materials of the new colony, as well as to display the artefacts made by the Maori people of New Zealand and the people of the Pacific Islands.

The Auckland Institute was founded in 1867 as a learned society and in 1868 became affiliated to the newly established New Zealand Institute, a scientific body modelled on the British Royal Society. The New Zealand Institute became the Royal Society of New Zealand in 1933, but the Auckland Institute retained its original title. Among the aims of the Auckland Institute was the establishment of a museum for the education of the public and objects were presented for that purpose at the very first meeting. In 1869, the Superintendent of the Auckland Province transferred the old 1852 Auckland Museum to the control of the Auckland Institute. The organisation subsequently became known as the Auckland Institute and Museum. In 1876, the Museum moved to new premises in Princes Street, near the present Hyatt Kingsgate Hotel.

At the end of the First World War, the citizens of Auckland agreed to erect a new building for the Museum as a memorial to those who had enlisted in the Auckland Province and been killed during the war. The Auckland War Memorial Museum was built on the hilltop site in the Domain where it stands today and opened in 1929. After the Second World War, the building was extended as a further memorial. The extension was opened in 1960 and completed by the addition of an auditorium in 1969. Thus the original Auckland Museum became part of the Auckland Institute and Museum, the local branch of the Royal Society of New Zealand, and is today housed in the Auckland War Memorial Museum building.

Auckland Institute and Museum, Princes Street 1876-1929

Maori and Pacific displays, Princes Street, about 1900

The Auckland Institute and Museum is administered by a Council of 29 members. Twelve members of the Council are elected by the 2000 Members (or "friends") of the Auckland Institute and Museum, three are elected by the Council itself, and fourteen are elected or appointed by the City, Borough and County Councils of the Auckland Region. About 75% of the Museum's annual operating budget is received from a levy on these local authorities. The remainder comes from endowments, gifts, grants and bequests, from the Museum Shop and Coffee Lounge and from donations. Less than 1% is received from the New Zealand Government, in the form of specific grants, though the Museum's education staff are employed by the Department of Education.

Opening the Auckland War Memorial Museum, November 28th 1929

Elders of many tribes reopen the house *Hotunui*, November 29th 1929

Stonemasons carve the War Memorial Museum columns about 1927

The Maori displays, Princes Street, about 1900

Te Pokiha Taranui of Ngati Pikiao named his large pataka *Puawai o Te Arawa (Flower of the Arawa)* to mark it as the finest pataka ever. It was carved for him by Wero about 1879, and was erected at Maketu in the Bay of Plenty. 151

MAORI

The ancestors of the Maori people arrived in New Zealand a thousand years ago. They came from the central eastern Pacific — perhaps Tahiti, perhaps the Cook Islands. Their ocean voyages were among the greatest feats of discovery and exploration of the age.

The land they discovered was huge, compared with their tiny island homes, and rich in natural resources. Great forests gave timber for housing and canoes, and plants for clothing, ropes and nets. Plentiful bird life, notably the many species of giant moa, and seas teeming with fish, marine mammals and other animals provided all their needs. Efficient tools and beautiful ornaments were made from previously unknown types of rock.

In this abundant environment, the Maori developed a society strongly based on the family, the tribe and the land. They also developed their art into many rich and varied forms, which often reflect their concern to establish who they are descended from and to whom they are related.

The art of the Maori is the visible expression of the history and the values of the family or tribe; the invisible, and richest portion is in the wisdom, the speech and the song of the elders and the people. Auckland Museum is proud to be able to display many of the great treasures of the Maori. Remember, however, that these things offer only a glimpse of the richness of the Maori world. When you look on these objects, think also of the people who made them.

Te Oha (The Abundant) is an appropriate name for a storehouse. The pataka was carved about 1825 by Manawa and Tahuriorangi, noted chiefs of Ngati Pikiao, using adzes of greenstone. It stood at Waerenga on Rotorua, just west of the Ohau Channel. 152

The figure above the doorway of the pataka *Puawai o Te Arawa* is identified as Tama te Kapua, captain of the Arawa canoe and founder of the whole Arawa people. 151

Poupou panel from the interior of *Hotunui* which represents the ancestor Ngahaupaha 49394 Taipari

The great carved house *Hotunui* was erected in 1878 at Parawai near Thames. It was carved as a wedding gift from Apanui Hamaiwaho of Ngati Awa of Whakatane to celebrate the marriage of his daughter Mereana Mokomoko to Hoterini Taipari of Ngati Maru of Thames.

Ngati Awa carvers, under the direction of Wepiha Apanui, carved the main panels of the house in Whakatane between 1875 and 1878. The carvings were then taken to Parawai and the house was completed — Hoterini Taipari carved the ridge pole himself. Following the style of Ngati Awa at that time the carvings were decorated in vivid red, white and black paint.

In 1924 the house was placed on loan in the Auckland Museum and substantial restoration undertaken of decayed or missing carvings and woven panels. As part of the restoration, the house was repainted in a monochrome red. A project is now underway to remove this red overpaint and restore the original colours.

49394 Taipari

6

This carving of Pukaki with his wife and two sons was part of the gateway to the pa at Te Ngae on the eastern shore of Rotorua in the early nineteenth century. Pukaki was a leading chief of the Arawa tribe in the seventeenth century.

161 Gillies

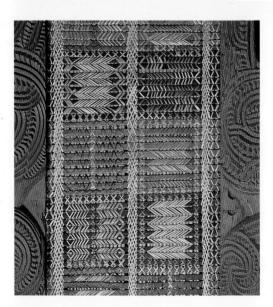

Detail of a woven tukutuku panel from the interior of *Hotunui*   49394 Taipari

A carved panel from *Te Potaka*.

22063 Spencer

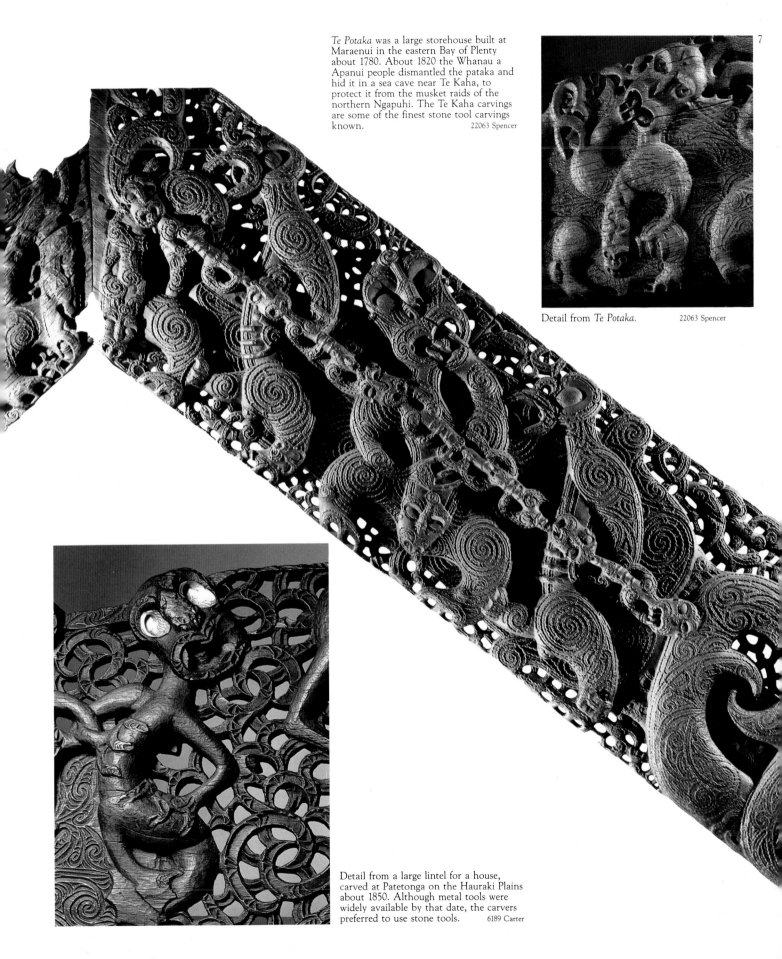

Te Potaka was a large storehouse built at Maraenui in the eastern Bay of Plenty about 1780. About 1820 the Whanau a Apanui people dismantled the pataka and hid it in a sea cave near Te Kaha, to protect it from the musket raids of the northern Ngapuhi. The Te Kaha carvings are some of the finest stone tool carvings known.   22063 Spencer

Detail from *Te Potaka*.   22063 Spencer

Detail from a large lintel for a house, carved at Patetonga on the Hauraki Plains about 1850. Although metal tools were widely available by that date, the carvers preferred to use stone tools.   6189 Carter

The Kaitaia carving was found buried in Lake Tangonge near Kaitaia in 1920. Its carving style has strong resemblance to tropical Polynesian forms and in many ways is quite unlike later Maori art. The central figure with flanking creatures is a motif found in many lintels in later periods, however. We believe that the carving was made early in the development of art in New Zealand, perhaps about 1300 A.D.   6341 Clark

Tauihu (prow carving) of *Te Toki a Tapiri*
150

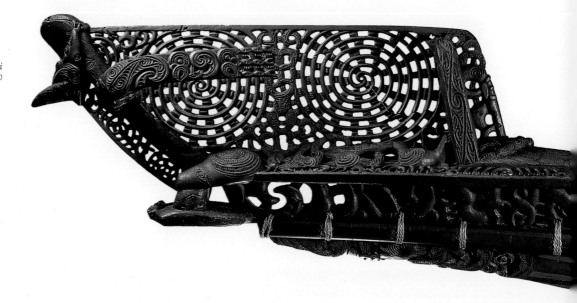

Te Toki a Tapiri is the last of the great Maori war canoes. It was built about 1836 for Te Waka Tarakau of Ngati Kahungunu, who lived near Wairoa in Hawkes Bay. Its name, *the battle-axe of Tapiri*, commemorates a famous ancestor of Tarakau. Tarakau presented the canoe as a gift to Te Waka Perohuka of the Rongowhakaata people of Poverty Bay. Perohuka and others carved the decoration on the canoe. In 1853 Perohuka presented the canoe to Ngapuhi chief Tamati Waka Nene and his brother Patuone to commemorate the end of the northern tribe's musket raids on the East Coast.

The canoe was brought to Auckland and sold to Kaihau and Te Katipa of Ngati Te Ata of Waiuku. In 1860, following the outbreak of war in the Waikato, Government forces seized the vessel, even though Ngati Te Ata had not taken part in the fighting. (Compensation was paid to Ngati Te Ata at the end of the war). An unsuccessful attempt was made to blow up the canoe while it lay on the beach at Onehunga. In 1869 the canoe was restored and used in a regatta on the Waitemata Harbour organised for the Duke of Edinburgh. Ngati Whatua of Orakei under Paora Tuhaere later looked after the canoe until it was presented to the Auckland Museum by the New Zealand Government in 1885. The canoe is 24 metres long and could carry a hundred men. 150

Taurapa (stern carving) of *Te Toki a Tapiri*
150

Rakaruhi Rukupo, a famous carver of the Rongowhakaata tribe of Gisborne, carved this model of a waka taua in the middle of the last century. 44117

The Maori migration from tropical Polynesia to temperate New Zealand required the development of more substantial clothing. The inner fibres of the New Zealand flax *Phormium tenax* were twisted into threads and hand tied to make warm and beautiful cloaks and other garments. Many varieties of cloaks were produced. Some were decorated by the inclusion of feathers or flax tags and these dress cloaks were worn by people of rank on top of a plainer cloak.

On a korowai cloak, short lengths of closely twisted flax dyed black are attached to the outside of the cloak.

27985 West

We do not know the name of the expert weaver of patterned baskets who created this flax kete whakairo at Kawhia before 1875.

294 Smales

Fine kaitaka cloaks with a geometric taniko border were sometimes worn with a feather cloak on top. The Ngapuhi chief Tamati Waka Nene presented this cloak to a pakeha friend in the Bay of Islands in the 1860s.

293 Barstow

The most highly valued cloak of all is the kahukura, covered entirely with red feathers from the kaka parrot *Nestor meridionalis*. This example was made by Makurata Paitini of Tuhoe about 1900.
5975 Brett

A dogskin cloak was the highly valued war cloak of a chief. Strips of the skin of the Maori dog were sewn onto the outside of the cloak.
280 Davis

In rain capes, sections of untreated flax or other leaf cover the outside of the cloak, to afford good protection from the weather.
1492 Grey

Cloak decorated with the feathers of the New Zealand pigeon *Hemiphaga novaeseelandiae*. The cloak was made by the Tuhoe people of the Urewera in the 1880s.
16110 Brett

12 In the South Island of New Zealand, the early Maori explorers discovered nephrite jade. This precious stone was highly prized for its hardness in tools and its beauty in ornaments. It was traded throughout the country.

The hei tiki, a jade pendant in human form, was rather rare in the eighteenth century but has become very fashionable since. This large example was probably collected in Dusky Sound in 1795.
3320 Vaile

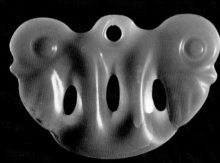

Pekapeka is the name of the native bat and it is also the name for a style of nephrite pendant. 30852

Precious valuables, like the feathers of the rare huia (now extinct) and jade ornaments, were kept in elaborately carved waka huia, hung from the rafters of a house.
31512 Oldman

The spiral, which is a feature of Maori woodcarving, is produced in jade in the pendant koropepe. This example is from Northland.
7150 Vaile

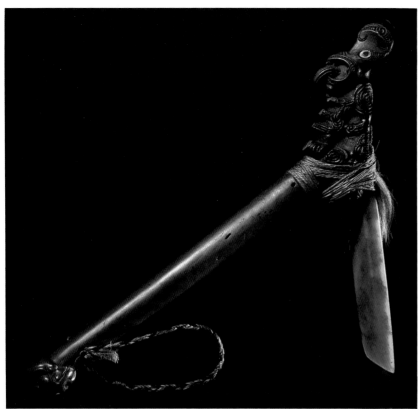

The hei matau is a nephrite pendant in the shape of a fish hook.   5586, 5598

The toki poutangata is the ceremonial adze of a chief, a visible sign of his rank and status. This toki poutangata named *Tawhaki* is an heirloom of the Mataatua peoples, handed down from Ngati Awa chief Te Apanui of Whakatane.   1999 Stewart

This mere pounamu belonged to Iwirakau, a famous ancestor of Ngati Porou.   505

The elegant kapeu was worn suspended from the ear.   5611

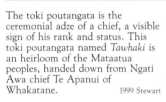

Adze-shaped pendant from Spirits Bay in Northland. Its beautiful jade is likened to the breast feathers of the shining cuckoo, pipiwharauroa.   6425 Vaile

Maori weapons were mostly stabbing, thrusting implements. They included short weapons for use in one hand (patu, wahaika, mere, kotiate describe different forms), and long weapons for two (taiaha, tewhatewha). There is no satisfactory word in English for these weapons — "club" is not correct.

Kotiate made from whalebone, with sealing wax inset into the eyes.   335 Davis

This basalt patu onewa belongs to the Kawerau tribe of Auckland and comes from Korekore pa at Muriwai on Auckland's West Coast.   34742

The hair of the Maori dog and the feathers of the kaka are used to decorate the head of a taiaha.   22491.4

The putorino is a trumpet like instrument, probably used for signalling.
36721 Vaile

Birds were stored for the winter in taha huahua, containers made from a gourd, with an ornately carved neck. The birds were preserved in their own fat.   835, 5176

Many varieties of fish hooks were used. These were made of wood or bone, or sometimes stone or shell. This wooden hook with a bone point was being used about 1800.   5977

Not all wooden floats for fishing nets were as elaborately carved as this float from Rotoiti.   40 Mair

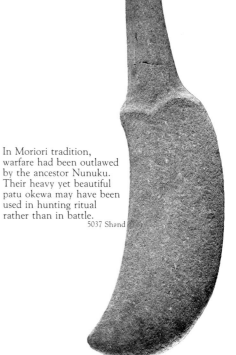

In Moriori tradition, warfare had been outlawed by the ancestor Nunuku. Their heavy yet beautiful patu okewa may have been used in hunting ritual rather than in battle.
5037 Shand

MORIORI

The Moriori people of the Chatham Islands were Polynesians, closely related to the Maori of New Zealand physically and in language, art and culture. However, in their isolated islands they developed distinctive forms of culture and dialect which clearly distinguish them from the mainland Maori. The last Moriori died in 1933, though many Chatham Islanders today claim descent from mixed Maori and Moriori ancestors.

This carving from Tupuangi in the Chatham Islands is the only Moriori wood sculpture in existence. It is thought to represent Hatitimatangi, a principal Moriori god.   18567 Ritchie

PACIFIC HALL

Auckland Museum's Pacific Hall displays the art and cultures of the peoples of the wide Pacific. The islands of the Pacific divide into three great cultural groups: Melanesia, "the black islands" in the west, extending from New Guinea to Fiji; Micronesia, "the small islands" in the north from the Marianas to Kiribati; and in the east Polynesia, "the many islands" lying in a triangle from Hawaii to Easter Island to New Zealand. All are represented here, except the Maori people of New Zealand, whose display galleries are adjacent. Particularly notable are the Polynesian displays, which is only fitting for the largest Polynesian city in the world.

MICRONESIA

In Kiribati, chiefs went to war protected in a suit of armour made from coconut fibre. This afforded them good protection from knives and swords edged with shark teeth.   13169 Ellis

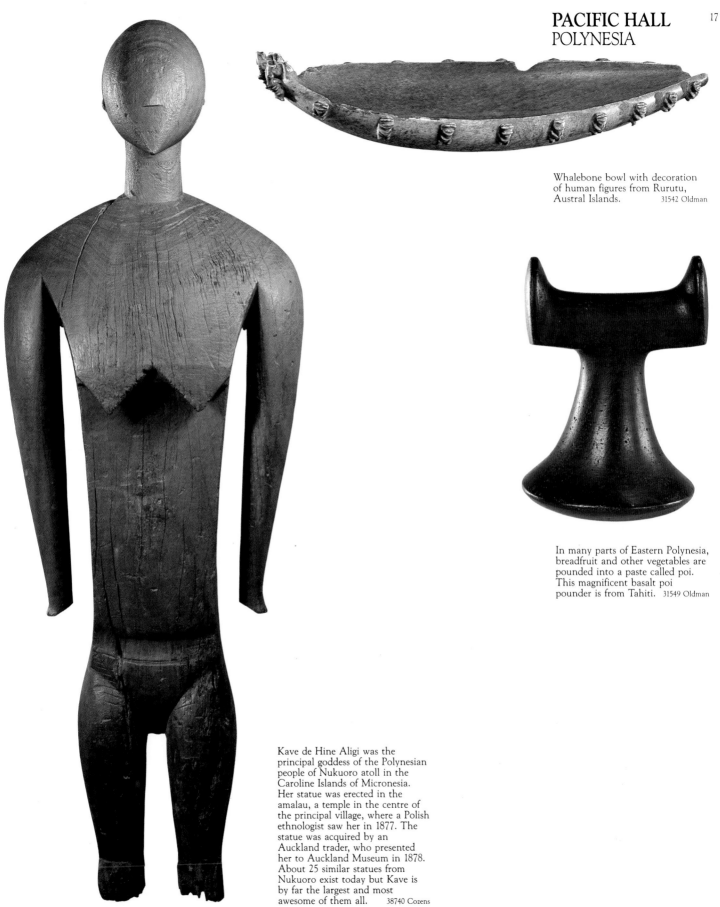

Whalebone bowl with decoration of human figures from Rurutu, Austral Islands.   31542 Oldman

In many parts of Eastern Polynesia, breadfruit and other vegetables are pounded into a paste called poi. This magnificent basalt poi pounder is from Tahiti. 31549 Oldman

Kave de Hine Aligi was the principal goddess of the Polynesian people of Nukuoro atoll in the Caroline Islands of Micronesia. Her statue was erected in the amalau, a temple in the centre of the principal village, where a Polish ethnologist saw her in 1877. The statue was acquired by an Auckland trader, who presented her to Auckland Museum in 1878. About 25 similar statues from Nukuoro exist today but Kave is by far the largest and most awesome of them all.   38740 Cozens

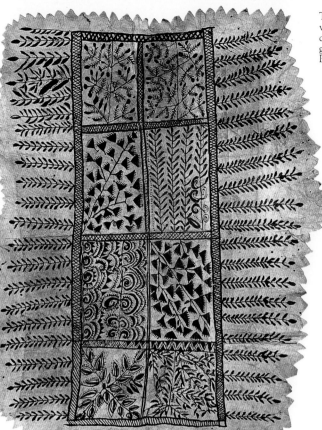

Tapa from Niue is often decorated in a very distinctive way, with beautiful floral designs. This piece was collected by the great Maori scholar, Te Rangi Hiroa (Sir Peter Buck).   999 Hiroa

In Tonga, figures which represent goddesses or perhaps important female ancestors were carved in wood and ivory. Auckland Museum has several outstanding examples. The ivory figure is carved from the tooth of a sperm whale. The wooden sculpture was collected by missionaries in 1830 at Lifuka in the Ha'apai Islands of Tonga. Both carvings were probably made in the eighteenth century.
31895, 32652 Oldman

Bark cloth is made all over the Pacific, from Indonesia to Hawaii to New Zealand. Different people call it by different names — masi, kapa, siapo, hiapo but a general word is tapa.

Samoan tapa printed with a carved wooden block and overpainted in black and brown.   52018

The principal gods of Rarotonga, Cook Islands, were represented by a carved staff over four metres long. Most of these god staffs were burned by nineteenth century Christian missionaries. A few complete small staffs survive, as well as portions of the larger ones.   31487 Oldman

The chiefly cloaks of Hawaii were decorated with the feathers of hundreds of birds. Only six or seven suitable yellow feathers could be obtained from each bird. This cloak dates from about the beginning of the nineteenth century. 29817

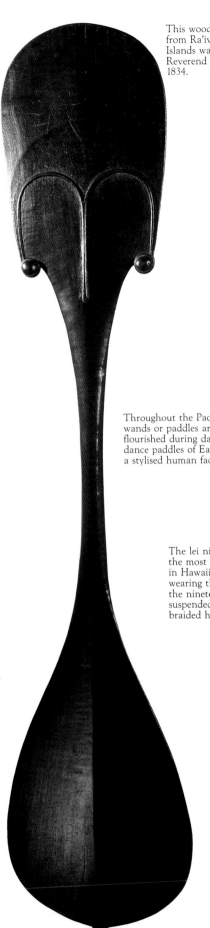

This wooden sculpture of a goddess from Ra'ivavae in the Austral Islands was taken to England by Reverend John Williams about 1834.   31499 Oldman

Throughout the Pacific, wooden wands or paddles are held and flourished during dancing. The dance paddles of Easter Island have a stylised human face and form.
31475 Oldman

The lei niho palaoa remains today the most valued chiefly ornament in Hawaii. The usual way of wearing the whale ivory hook in the nineteenth century was suspended from a necklet of braided human hair.   16319.1 Shirrifs

PACIFIC HALL
MELANESIA

As part of the New Ireland malanggan ceremonies carvings of birds struggling with snakes were displayed together with those of the ancestors. 4365 McGregor

In western New Ireland, Papua New Guinea, carved malanggan figures represented a dead person in memorial services. Malanggan ceremonies were an important part of New Ireland life, when the dead were farewelled and new adults were initiated. 4364.2-4 McGregor

In eastern New Ireland, Papua New Guinea, chalk figures commemorated dead relations. After the funeral ceremonies, the figure was broken to let the spirit go free to join the ancestors, unless the carving was collected by a missionary, as this one was about 1890. 11559 Brown

Wooden shield from the
village of Motu Motu, near
Port Moresby, Papua New
Guinea.   15463 Leys

Decorated earthenware pot
collected by an Auckland
Museum expedition in
Zumin Village, Upper
Markham River, Papua New
Guinea, in 1972.   46102 Vaile

Men's houses of the Sepik river, Papua
New Guinea, were used to hold the sacred
symbols of the ancestral spirits, for use in
religious ceremonies. Food was hung from
the rafters of the house on specially
decorated hooks.   9200, 9194

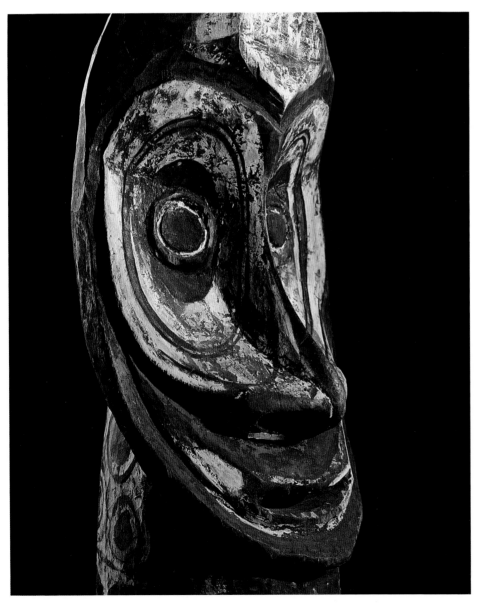

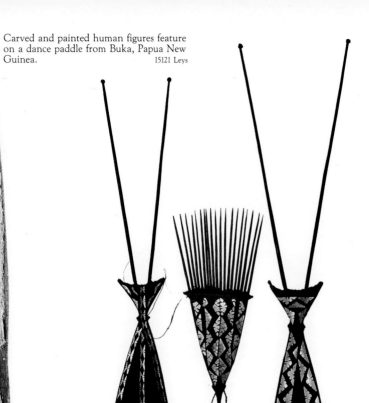

Carved and painted human figures feature on a dance paddle from Buka, Papua New Guinea.　　　　　15121 Leys

Decorative hair combs, Solomon Islands. Mother of pearl pieces have been inlaid into a resin coating on the palm wood combs.　　28078.1, 32345.2 & 8　Palmer, Vaile

Basketry shield from Nggela Island, in the southern Solomon Islands, used more in ceremonies than in war.　　2813 Kinder

The frigate bird was respected in the Solomon Islands for its ability to catch fish. Frigate birds and fish are shown on this pearl shell ornament from Roviana, Solomon Islands, which was hung in the stern of a canoe to ensure fair weather.
15228 Leys

Fijian priests had special bowls for both the oil they used for anointing and also their special stimulating yaqona drink.   31541 Oldman

Six pieces of whale tooth ivory form the border to this pearl shell breast ornament from Fiji.
31498 Oldman

In many Melanesian religions masks are worn to represent the spirits of ancestors. These spirits, sometimes kind but more often harmful, needed to be driven from the village as the culmination of a ceremony. This mask from New Caledonia represents the spirit of an ancestor.
18208

Tumbuan dance mask of the Siassi people of western New Britain, Papua New Guinea. A dancer wearing the mask represented the spirit of an ancestor.
25536 Armitage

Canoe prow figure from
Bougainville, Solomon Islands
(today part of Papua New
Guinea). These nguzunguzu
figures were lashed to the prows
of the war canoes when the
warriors set out on a raid.
Today they are a popular craft
product of the Solomons.
15277 Leys

PACIFIC CANOES

The peoples of the Pacific have always been great
sailors and navigators. They use their canoes for
transport, to take them fishing and to carry their
trade. Pacific canoes have a grace and beauty
that is unique.

Outrigger attachment detail on
Te Ingoa o Pu, the sailing canoe
from Tikopia, which was made
about 1900.   12992 Wood

HALL OF MAN

The way of life of many different peoples is the subject of this display. Human evolution and the development of civilisations are described, as well as the lifestyles of several small scale societies.

The Dyaks of Borneo are an agricultural people living in communal long houses in their isolated jungle villages.

The fashion in Athens in the sixth century B.C. was to decorate wine jugs like this with scenes painted in black on a red background. On this jug Hercules fights with the Amazons. 29699 Mackelvie

The woman whose mummified body is in the carved coffin lived in Egypt during the 18th Dynasty, about 1500 B.C.   52021

Portrait from the coffin of a woman who lived in Fayoum, Egypt, about the time of Cleopatra, in the first century B.C.   22218 Hoffman

The Ashanti people of Nigeria used gold dust as money, with brass weights to measure the gold. In the nineteenth century brass-figures based on the weights were often made for sale to Europeans.
34771.1-2 Powell

Men in the Kimberley Plateau of northern Australia wear pendants intricately carved from pearl shell.   7769 Hemingway

Shadow puppets from Java, Indonesian ship models 29 and containers from Java, Sumatra and Burma feature in the display of Arts and Crafts of Southeast Asia.

The American Indians of the Central Plains hunted herds of buffalo on the prairies and grew crops in their gardens.

The pre-Columbian goldsmiths of Central and South America were masters of their art, casting gold into many wonderful forms. This frog was made in Panama between 1000 and 1500 A.D. It was obtained in Panama in 1868 by New Zealand Governor Sir George Grey. For security reasons, only a copy is on display.   26436 Grey

ASIA

The Hall of Asian Art shows the richness and variety
of the cultures of Asia, from neolithic China to the
T'ang, Sung and Ming periods, from Turkey and Iran
in the West to Korea, Japan and Southeast Asia.

The eastward expansion of the Greek Empire, and
the westward expansion of Indian kings and rulers
resulted in a blending of art styles. This schist
statue of the Buddha was sculpted in the
Gandhara a region of North West India in the
second or third century A.D.   M1067 Mackelvie

Nineteenth century Japanese ivory netsuke, a toggle used to fasten a container to the belt.
M155 Mackelvie

Jade water buffalo from the Chinese Emperor's Summer Palace in Beijing, probably dating from the Sung Dynasty (960 — 1279 A.D.). Presented to the Museum by Sir George Grey. J17 Grey

A lohan is a follower of the Buddha, who through study and meditation has become so enlightened that he may enter Nirvana directly when he dies without another re-birth. This wooden sculpture of a lohan was carved in China early in the Ming Dynasty, about 1400 A.D. Traces of its painted decoration may still be seen. M1036 Humphreys-Davies

Chinese porcelain figurine of the Buddhist deity Kuan yin, Ming Dynasty (1368-1644 A.D.)
K4785

Detail of cranes from a nineteenth century
Japanese silk robe. Only a few Asian textiles are on
display at a time, to help preserve them. T663 Disney

Gold lacquer box made in the Edo period of Japan
(1615 — 1868 A.D.). Presented by the late James
Mackelvie. The Trust he established continues to
add to his collections in Auckland Museum and
the Auckland City Art Gallery. M705 Mackelvie

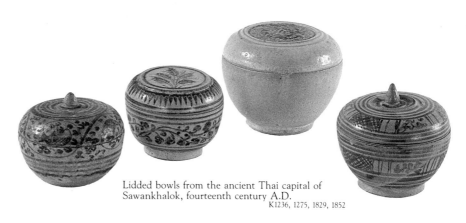

Lidded bowls from the ancient Thai capital of
Sawankhalok, fourteenth century A.D.
K1236, 1275, 1829, 1852

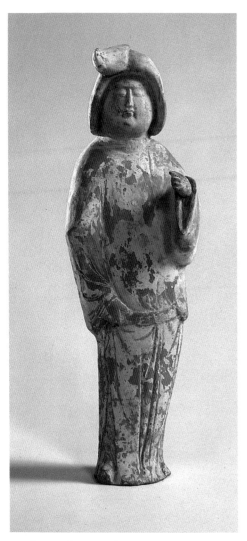

In China in the T'ang dynasty (618 — 960 A.D.),
pottery figures like this court lady were buried in
the graves of wealthy people.   K1776 Humphreys-Davies

Indonesia and Malaysia are renowned for the
quality of their silver wares.   S508, S510 Alma-Baker

A hill, symbolising the Taoist paradise, features on
Hill Jars from Han Dynasty China (206 B.C. —
220 A.D.)   K2788 Clark

Celadon glazed wine pot
from the Koryö dynasty
of Korea (918-1392 A.D.)
K2386 Rule

APPLIED ARTS
POTTERY

The Museum's displays in the Logan Campbell Gallery show the development of European and especially English pottery. New Zealand studio pottery is also displayed here.

The Gallery is named in honour of a founder of Auckland whose estate continues to support the work of the Museum.

Lambeth charger with the arms of the Guild of Cutlers, and the date 1650. Its design copies a painting by Titian.   K1751

A wooden comb was trailed through a slip coating to decorate this Staffordshire platter in about 1700.   K1092

Thomas Whieldon of Staffordshire made this teapot with its distinctive glaze about 1760.   K1093

Hispano-Moresque pottery was developed after the Catholic conquest of Muslim Spain in the fourteenth century A.D. This piece was made about 1700.   K1104

Jasper ware urn made in Staffordshire about 1790, imitating the work of Josiah Wedgwood.   K1035 Vaile

Introducing tobacco into the glaze produced the pattern on this Mocha ware tea pot, made in Staffordshire about 1820.   K1102

Chelsea figurine of Venus and Cupid made about 1760. It has the distinctive Gold Anchor mark on the back. K663 White

Len Castle was one of the founders of the
Studio Pottery movement in New Zealand
in the 1950s. He made this platter in 1976.
K3123 Castle

APPLIED ARTS
NEW ZEALAND CRAFTS

Contemporary craft is a rapidly growing area of our
displays. The collection documents the development of
many craft forms, in New Zealand and other parts of
the world, in pottery, glass, jewellery, and textiles.

Cecilia Parkinson of Auckland made this
vase in 1982.
K4198 Disney

Gary Nash of Auckland ground and cut
this blown glass form in 1984.   G420 Disney

Auckland glass artist Peter Viesnik made
this plate in 1984.
G422 Viesnik

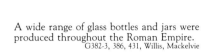

A wide range of glass bottles and jars were produced throughout the Roman Empire.
G382-3, 386, 431, Willis, Mackelvie

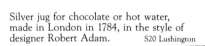

Silver jug for chocolate or hot water, made in London in 1784, in the style of designer Robert Adam. S20 Lushington

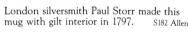

London silversmith Paul Storr made this mug with gilt interior in 1797. S182 Allen

APPLIED ARTS
SILVER

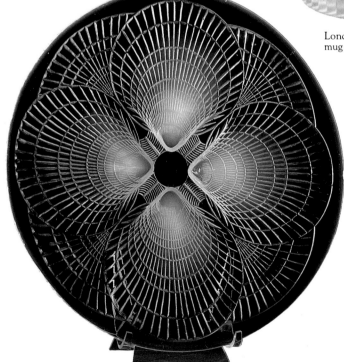

René Lalique was the foremost Art Deco designer in France when he made this glass plate in the 1920s. G292

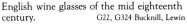

English wine glasses of the mid eighteenth century. G22, G324 Bucknill, Lewin

APPLIED ARTS
ENGLISH FURNITURE

The Charles Disney Hall of English Furniture
commemorates the generosity of this benefactor of the
Museum. The Disney Art Trust he established provides
a continuing source of income for the purchase of
applied arts objects for the Museum.

Robert Adam was influenced by the French in his
1775 design for a Neo-classical chair with gilt wood
arms and oval back.   F141 Mackelvie

This walnut jewel cabinet with pewter
inlay on the doors was made about 1690,
in William and Mary style.   F19 Mappin

Mahogany cabinet designed in England
about 1750 by Thomas Chippendale in his
"Chinese" manner.   F12

Pewter is an alloy of tin with copper or
lead. These German and English pieces
range in date from 1619 to 1790.
P43-4, 47, 64, 101 Fenton

CENTENNIAL STREET

Centennial Street gives an impression of Auckland's Queen Street in 1866. One of the shops represented is the drapers and milliners establishment of Milne and Choyce, a company which celebrated its centennial in 1966 and was the sponsor of this whole exhibit.

The shops and businesses, the house and the hotel are all furnished in the style of the day. They contain a wide variety of articles and implements in use in colonial Auckland of the nineteenth century.

The chemist's shop window of the Apothecaries' Hall of J.C. Sharland.

Henry Niccol was in business as a ship chandler, supplying nautical goods, between about 1843 and 1870.

German settlers Berwin and Mendelsson operated a tobacconists' shop in Queen Street in 1866.

HALLS OF MEMORY

The Auckland War Memorial Museum was built and extended as a memorial to those men and women who enlisted in the Auckland Province and were killed in two World Wars: 7,297 names are inscribed in the World War One Hall of Memories, and 4,702 in the Hall of Memories for World War Two. More broadly, however, the building stands as a living memorial to all those who have died in conflict throughout our nation's history. The Museum's displays of military history serve to illustrate and perhaps explain the sacrifice they made.

The stained glass window in the World War Two Hall of Memories was designed by Mr F.V. Ellis, and made at Miller Studios, Dunedin.

The coloured glass leadlight ceiling over the entrance foyer contains the crests of Great Britain and her Dominions and Colonies involved in the First World War. Clockwise from the three lions in the Northwest corner the countries represented are: Jersey and Guernsey, Fiji, Jamaica, Malta, Gibraltar, Kenya, South Africa, Newfoundland, Canada, Great Britain, New Zealand, Australia, India, Ceylon, Malaya and the Straits Settlements. The ceiling was designed by the architects of the Museum, Grierson, Aimer and Draffin.

The New Zealand Cross is one of the world's rarest military decorations: only twenty three were ever awarded. The Auckland Museum example was awarded to Cornet H.C.W. Wrigg for his actions at Opotiki in 1867.　N2715

MILITARY HISTORY

Air Chief Marshal Sir Keith Park, New Zealand's most distinguished airman of World War Two, arranged for the Supermarine Spitfire Mark XVI to be presented to the Museum in 1956.　W1263

The Mitsubishi A6M Zero was the outstanding Japanese fighter aeroplane of the Second World War. Very few survive. Auckland Museum's A6M3 Zero Model 22 was taken by New Zealand forces in New Britain in 1945.　W2914

The Museum has an extensive range of military uniforms from the eighteenth century to the present day. Those on display are changed periodically. This is a Colonel's dress jacket of the reign of George V.　U107

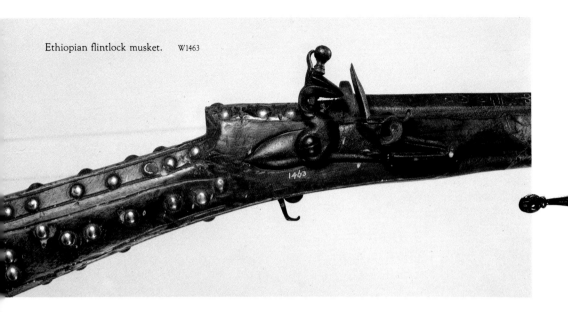

Ethiopian flintlock musket.   W1463

Bedouin matchlock musket, with
inlaid gold and silver decoration.
W1507

Japanese matchlock musket.
W1513 Dadley

Victorian dress sword.
W1301 Harris

Nineteenth century
Naval Officer's
sword.
W1451.2

MARITIME

This hall illustrates New Zealand's place as a maritime nation. It is envisaged that the collection will transfer to the Auckland Maritime Museum being developed on the waterfront.

The historic whale boat *Tainui* was built in New Bedford, U.S.A. in the early nineteenth century. In 1868 she was brought to New Zealand and was used extensively in shore whaling throughout northern New Zealand until 1903.　　Mar408 McIntosh

Carving on ivory, especially the teeth of the sperm whale, was a popular sailor's art in the nineteenth century. It was called scrimshaw.　　Mar18

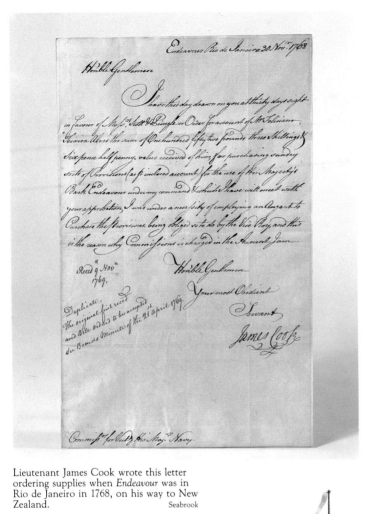

Lieutenant James Cook wrote this letter ordering supplies when *Endeavour* was in Rio de Janeiro in 1768, on his way to New Zealand.   Seabrook

Figurehead from the Craig Shipping Line barque *Hazel Craig*, built in Aberdeen in 1879.   Mar213 Lady Richmond

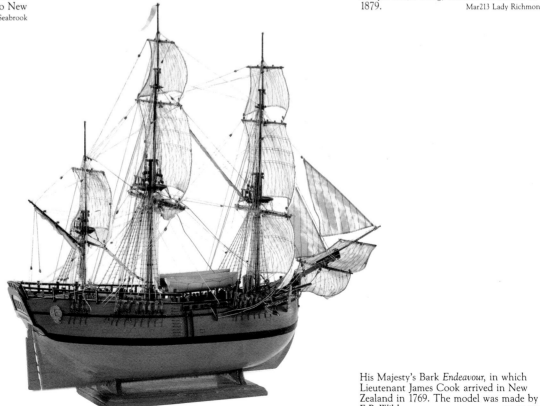

His Majesty's Bark *Endeavour*, in which Lieutenant James Cook arrived in New Zealand in 1769. The model was made by E.P. Wild.   Mar39 Wild

NATURAL HISTORY
NEW ZEALAND BIRDS

Over three hundred species of birds live in New Zealand, or have done so in the past. Of the birds which are now extinct, the best known is the Moa but many different birds have disappeared through the effects of human beings on our land. Some of our native birds are endangered species and considerable efforts are being made to try to ensure their survival.

New Zealand's many estuaries and lagoons provide rich food resources for many wading birds. Our display shows bar-tailed godwits, wrybills, turnstones, a knot and a sandpiper.

The flightless Takahe *Notornis mantelli* was believed to have become extinct in the nineteenth century. A small population, now numbering about 120 birds, was discovered in Fiordland in 1948.

There were many species of Moa — the Museum displays the skeletons of several, and a reconstruction of the largest of them all, standing some four metres tall. *Dinornis maximus* became extinct about 1500 A.D., after being extensively hunted by the early Maori settlers. The last of the smaller Moa probably died about 1800 A.D.

The Australasian Bittern *Botaurus stellaris* is one of New Zealand's many birds of lakes, swamps and streams.

The Brown Kiwi *Apteryx australis* is the commonest of the three species of Kiwi. The Kiwi has short stumpy wings but cannot fly. It feeds at night on insects on the forest floor, using its long bill and good sense of smell to find food.

NATURAL HISTORY
AUCKLAND LANDSCAPES

This display illustrating the physical setting of Auckland has as a central feature a working model of the island volcano Rangitoto which dominates the Auckland skyline. Its eruption about 1350 A.D. buried a Maori village on the neighbouring island Motutapu.

The Atlas Moth *Attacus edwardsii*
of India and the Morpho Butterfly
Morpho anaxibia of Brazil. The
Atlas Moth's colour is created by
pigment in the wings, but the
Morpho Butterfly's blue colour is
caused by the refraction of light.

NATURAL HISTORY
INSECTS

The Giant Weta is now found
mostly on offshore islands; this
species, *Deinacrida fallai*, is found
only on the Poor Knights Islands.
The female has a body up to 10cm
long (this one is a male).

The New Zealand Red Admiral
butterfly *Bassaris gonerilla* is unique
to New Zealand.

A wing span up to 15cm makes the
Puriri Moth *Aenetus virescens* the
largest New Zealand moth.

In Victorian times collecting native ferns and making fern albums was a popular pastime. This specimen is the Hen and Chickens fern *Asplenium bulbiferum*.

Wardrobe of New Zealand native woods made about 1880 by William Norrie. The main timber is mottled kauri *Agathis australis* with many other timbers used for the geometric panels.

NATURAL HISTORY
BOTANY

The Cheeseman Herbarium in the Auckland Museum is one of the major museum collections of plants in this part of the world. Its collections are not very suitable for display, but they are used daily in the plant identification and research work of the Museum staff and many visiting scientists from New Zealand and overseas. The herbarium is named for Thomas Cheeseman, the Museum's curator from 1874 to 1924.

The New Zealand Kauri *Agathis australis* is one of the largest trees in the world and some specimens have lived over 2,000 years. Kauri gum was greatly prized in the nineteenth and early twentieth century for the manufacture of paints and varnishes. Particularly large or attractive pieces were sometimes polished and kept for their beauty.

The Scorpion Fish *Scorpaena cardinalis* hides on the sea floor, to lie in wait for its prey. It is found throughout New Zealand waters.

The Porcupine Fish *Allomycterus jaculiferus* can inflate its body with water to make it unattractive to predators.

The Red or Golden Snapper Centroberyx affinis lives in moderately deep water and feeds at night.

NATURAL HISTORY
FISHES

New Zealand waters are rich in fish and our display shows many species, some common and others quite unusual.

Red Moki *Cheilodactylus spectabilis* live in rocky reef areas, mostly in northern New Zealand. Large fish grow to over 60cm in length.

The Lancetfish *Alepisaurus ferox* is a voracious carnivore which hunts all kinds of smaller fishes, including smaller Lancetfish.

The New Zealand Paua *Haliotis iris* is related to the abalone of North America and Japan. Its dark flesh is prized as a food by many New Zealanders, while its iridescent shell has long been used to provide eyes for Maori carvings.

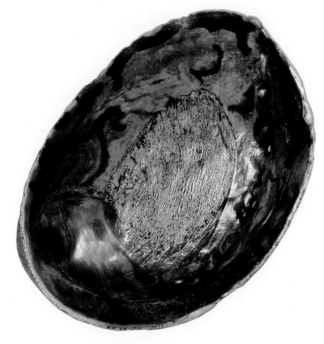

The female Paper Nautilus *Argonauta nodosa* grows a shell 23cm long to house her eggs, while the shell-less male grows to only 3cm. *Argonauta nodosa* is a relative of the octopus.

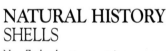

This New Zealand mountain snail *Paryphanta superba* is a large snail unique to New Zealand which eats mostly worms.

NATURAL HISTORY
SHELLS

New Zealand waters contain many species of shells, both marine and fresh water, while several species of native land snails are also found here.

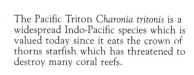

The Pacific Triton *Charonia tritonis* is a widespread Indo-Pacific species which is valued today since it eats the crown of thorns starfish which has threatened to destroy many coral reefs.

MUSEUM LIBRARY

The Library of the Auckland Institute and Museum is one of the three major scientific and historical reference libraries in New Zealand. Its wide ranging collections include books and periodicals on all subjects related to the Museum. Special collections include photographs, manuscripts, historical paintings, rare books and maps. The Library is open to the public for research.

A sketch by Charles Heaphy is one of the historical and topographical paintings and drawings in the Museum Library.

Rare books in the Museum Library.

MUSEUM SHOP

The Museum Shop offers an excellent range of hand made craft items, and hand carvings in jade, wood, flax and bone. Books and postcards relating to the Museum collections may be found here, as well as many other interesting and attractive items.

COFFEE LOUNGE

The Museum Coffee Lounge provides a pleasant place for the visitor to take a rest and enjoy some delicious refreshments.

SPECIAL EXHIBITIONS

A continually changing programme of Special Exhibitions is a major attraction at the Museum. This exhibition was "Musical Instruments Through the Ages", showing instruments from private collections as well as the Museum's own.

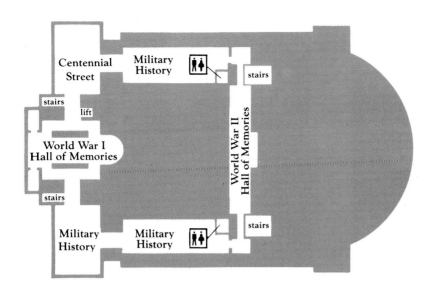

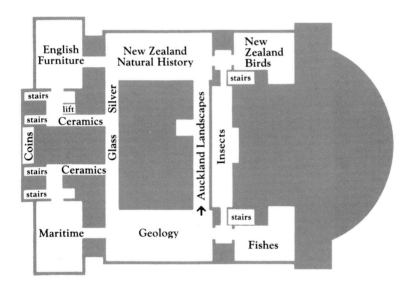

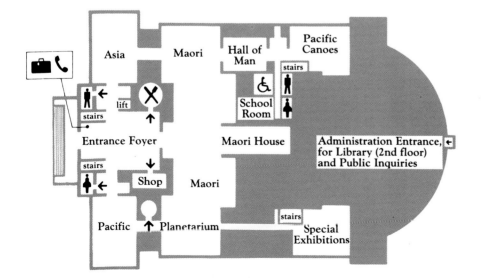

Plan of Display Galleries

SECOND FLOOR

Centennial Street
Halls of Memory
Military History

FIRST FLOOR

Auckland Landscapes
Ceramics, Glass & Silver
Coins
English Furniture
Geology
Insects
Maritime
New Zealand Birds
New Zealand Natural History
Fishes

GROUND FLOOR

Asia
Hall of Man
Maori
Pacific
Pacific Canoes
Special Exhibitions

Coffee Lounge
Museum Shop
School Room
Planetarium

Auckland Museum is open from 10am to 5pm daily, and is open every day of the year except Christmas Day and Good Friday.